# COUNTRIES OF THE WORLD

# *Ola,*
# BRAZIL

by Corey Anderson

CHERRY LAKE PUBLISHING · ANN ARBOR, MICHIGAN

Published in the United States of America by Cherry Lake Publishing
Ann Arbor, Michigan
www.cherrylakepublishing.com

Reading Adviser: Marla Conn MS, Ed., Literacy specialist, Read-Ability, Inc.

Book Design: Book Buddy Media

Photo Credits: ©StockSnap/Pixabay, cover (bottom), ©belterz/GettyImages, cover (top), ©12019/Pixabay, 1, ©iStockphoto/ Getty Images, 3, ©Pintai Suchachaisri/Getty Images, 4, ©Renata Souza e Souza/Getty Images, 5, ©FrankRamspott/Getty Images, 6, ©Matthew Stockman/Getty Images, 7 (top), ©tatosievers/Pixabay, 7 (bottom), ©FG Trade/Getty Images, 8, ©mantaphoto/Getty Images, 9, ©iStockphoto/Getty Images, 10, ©Photo Patrick Altmann/Getty Images, 11, ©Gabrielle Therin-Weise/Getty Images, 12, ©The Photographer/Wikimedia, 13, ©iStockphoto/Getty Images, 14, ©paul mansfield photography/Getty Images, 15, ©Ricardo Lima/Getty Images, 16, ©Igor Alecsander/Getty Images, 17, ©iStockphoto/ Getty Images, 18, ©Ricardo Moraes-Pool/Getty Images, 19, ©Jean Baptiste Debret/Wikimedia, 20, ©Mario Tama/Getty Images, 21, ©Brasil2/Getty Images, 22, ©FG Trade/Getty Images, 23, ©Danilo Borges/copa2014.gov.br/Wikimedia, 24, ©Jaim Simoes Oliveira/Getty Images, 25, ©Caiaimage/Getty Images, 26, ©Ana Lima/Getty Images, 27, ©sasint/ Pixabay, 28, ©Pete Norton/Getty Images, 29, ©Global_Pics/Getty Images, 30, ©Antonello/Getty Images, 31, ©SofiaV/ Shutterstock, 32, ©Andre Luiz Moreira/Shutterstock, 33, ©Joa Souza/Shutterstock, 34, ©PeopleImages/Getty Images, 35, ©J.Castro/Getty Images, 36, ©andresr/Getty Images, 38, ©Sylvain Grandadam/Getty Images, 39, ©Maarten Zeehandelaar/Shutterstock, 40, ©Aurora Open/Getty Images, 41 (bottom right), ©marianatavares.com/Getty Images, 41 (top), ©Ricardo Lima/Getty Images, 41 (bottom left), ©tmalucelli/Shutterstock, 42, ©Alexandre Camilo Bonato/ Shutterstock, 43, ©EyeEm/Getty Images, 44, ©Craig Hastings/Getty Images, 45, ©filo/Getty Images, background

Library of Congress Cataloging-in-Publication Data has been filed and is available at catalog.loc.gov

Cherry Lake Publishing would like to acknowledge the work of The Partnership for 21st Century Learning.
Please visit www.p21.org for more information.

Printed in the United States of America
Corporate Graphics

# TABLE OF CONTENTS

# CHAPTER 1

# WELCOME TO BRAZIL!

*Rio de Janeiro was the capital of Brazil from 1763 to 1960.*

The fifth-largest country in the world, Brazil is a land of lush rainforests, rugged coastlines, wetlands, and bustling towns. Brazil is slightly smaller than the United States, but is the largest country in South America. In fact, it is so huge, it shares borders with 10 other countries across the continent! A dream for city dwellers and nature lovers alike, Brazil is famous for its biodiversity. This means that a dazzling variety of mammal, bird, fish, and insect species live there. From toucans and jaguars to armadillos and anacondas, some of the Earth's most exotic creatures are found in Brazil.

*Toco toucans use their large bills to reach for fruit on tree branches, and to remove the fruit's skin.*

# ACTIVITY

Brazil is made up of 26 states. There is also one **federal** district, which is where you'll find Brasília, the capital. Using a separate sheet of paper, trace the map. Use an atlas or find a map online and label each of the 26 states and Brasília. Do you notice that some states are small while others are large? Why do you think this might be?

Brazil is home to some of South America's biggest cities, including São Paulo, a **landlocked** metropolis filled with skyscrapers, shops, restaurants, and millions of cars. It is one of the most populated cities on Earth. Rio de Janeiro, Belo Horizonte, and Brasília are also famous cities in Brazil. Nicknamed the "Marvelous City," Rio de Janeiro is well known for its beaches, green mountainsides, and samba music.

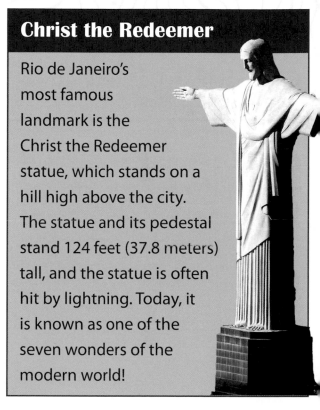

## Christ the Redeemer

Rio de Janeiro's most famous landmark is the Christ the Redeemer statue, which stands on a hill high above the city. The statue and its pedestal stand 124 feet (37.8 meters) tall, and the statue is often hit by lightning. Today, it is known as one of the seven wonders of the modern world!

*Street art is legal in Rio de Janeiro. Artists use colorful paint to decorate walls, columns, and other structures throughout the city.*

The different regions of Brazil each have unique landscapes and attractions. The north is known for its rugged natural features, including the second-longest river in the world, the Amazon. The largest rainforest on Earth is also called the Amazon and is located in the northern part of Brazil. It is more than 4,000 miles (6,400 kilometers) long. In the south, cowboys called gauchos herd cattle. An area called the Pantanal, the world's biggest wetlands, is located in Brazil's central western region. Wetlands are areas covered by marshes. Many people live in the southeast, which is home to some of Brazil's most crowded cities, including São Paulo, Rio de Janeiro, and Belo Horizonte.

*About 20,000 different types of plants can be found in the Amazon rainforest.*

## Iguaza Falls

On the border of Argentina and Brazil is the majestic Iguazu Falls. It is the largest waterfall system in the world, with more than 275 waterfalls spanning 1.7 miles (2.7 km). At 169 feet (51.5 m) high, Iguazu Falls is even taller than as Niagara Falls!

Most of Brazil lies in the Southern Hemisphere. That means it is winter from June through September, and it is summer from December through March. Brazil's climate can be very different in places, depending on the region and time of year.

Rainforests in Brazil are very hot and humid. Frequent showers during the wet season keep the rainforests healthy. In São Paulo and Rio de Janeiro, it is often scorching hot in the summertime. But it stays mild in the winter, with low temperatures at night sometimes dipping to around 65 degrees Fahrenheit (18 degrees Celsius).

*The Brazilian state of Minas Gerais is famous for being a source of gemstones, including aquamarine, amethyst, and topaz.*

*When Portuguese settlers arrived at this seaside city, they exclaimed "O, linda!" This means "Oh, beautiful!" in Portuguese. The city is now called Olinda.*

Although much of Brazil is **uninhabited**, it is home to some of the most crowded cities in the world, including São Paolo and Rio de Janeiro. Both cities deal with **overpopulation**. This can contribute to issues like crime and poverty. Brazil also struggles to control harmful **deforestation**. That means Brazil's rainforests are being cut down by humans, which can hurt the environment.

## Macaw Star

In the animated movie *Rio*, the main character is a Spix macaw, a strikingly bright blue parrot. Today, the Spix macaw has been declared **extinct** in the wild, though some still live in captivity. Scientists blame the beautiful bird's extinction on the clearing of Brazilian forests, which were their home. Of eight bird species recently discovered to be extinct, four of them lived in Brazil.

Controlling deforestation is important in order to protect the many different trees and creatures that live in Brazilian rainforests. Between August 2017 and July 2018, approximately 3,050 square miles (7,900 square kilometers) of Brazil's rainforests were destroyed. That's an area larger than the state of Delaware. It's also estimated that half of the tree species in the Amazon rainforest are now endangered. Scientists believe thousands of different mammal, bird, and insect species might also disappear forever because their habitat is being destroyed by humans.

*A jaguar's black spots are called rosettes because they resemble the shape of roses.*

# CHAPTER 2

# BUSINESS AND GOVERNMENT IN BRAZIL

For most of the country's history, many people in Brazil were farmers. They earned money by growing crops. In the 1900s, the country's economy grew when **manufacturing** was introduced. Companies began producing things like cars, airplanes, and clothing. Today, many people in Brazil work in service jobs as teachers, police officers, and cooks.

## Brazil's Economy

Economy means how a country makes and spends money. Brazil has the eighth-largest economy in the world and the biggest economy in South America. Brazil suffered a recession in recent years, which means its economy was struggling. Problems like unemployment are common during a recession.

*A coffee bean is actually the seed of the cherry-like fruit that grows on coffee plants.*

About 10 percent of Brazilians are farmers, who grow food for others to enjoy. Some crops remain in Brazil, while others are shipped all over the world. Crops that are grown in Brazil include coffee, sugarcane, citrus, and soybeans. Brazil is the second-largest producer of soybeans after the United States.

To export something means to send it to another country for its citizens to use. Sugar and poultry are some of Brazil's most popular food exports. Brazil is also the top exporter of orange juice in the world. Besides food, Brazil exports many other types of products, including iron ore and cars.

*Brazil produces about 35 percent of the world's oranges.*

## WHERE BRAZIL EXPORTS MOST OF ITS PRODUCTS:

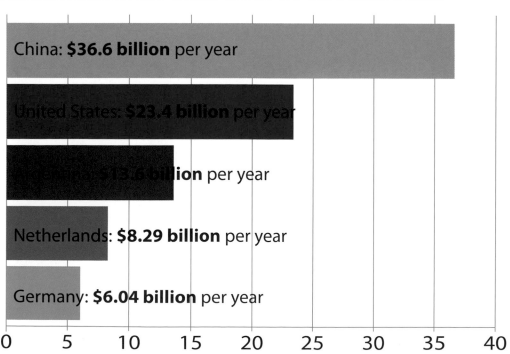

China: **$36.6 billion** per year

United States: **$23.4 billion** per year

Argentina: **$13.6 billion** per year

Netherlands: **$8.29 billion** per year

Germany: **$6.04 billion** per year

0    5    10    15    20    25    30    35    40

*In the city of Santarém, the port is equipped to load soybeans and other exports onto ships.*

Oil is Brazil's top import, followed by machinery, such as computers, and then passenger cars. Nearly 40 percent of products that Brazil imports from other countries come from Asia. Brazil also imports nearly $924 million in beverages from the United States alone!

Jobs in Brazil vary quite a bit, with some people working in offices while others work in the fields. Almost 60 percent of the people working in Brazil have jobs across the service industries, while nearly 10 percent of Brazilians still make a living through agriculture. The rest of the working population have jobs in mining, manufacturing, and construction.

*Many different crops are grown in Brazil, such as chives, corn, okra, and sweet potatoes.*

# ACTIVITY

Bar graphs are a good way to compare different values. Make a bar graph to show how many people have jobs related to agriculture, making a product, or providing a service. Ask an adult for help if you need it. Use the percentages mentioned in this chapter. Which bars will be similar in size? Which bar will be more than three times taller than the other two?

*The current president of Brazil, Jair Bolsonaro, served in the Brazilian army for 17 years.*

The Brazilian government has changed a lot throughout its history. Today, the government is a republic. Like the United States, Brazil's president is elected by voters.

## President Bolsonaro

In 2018, Brazil elected Jair Bolsonaro to be president. His opponents worry that his sometimes-controversial views on many issues might mean trouble for the nation. Opponents of Bolsonaro are particularly worried that he won't protect the environment or preserve Brazilians' human rights.

*In 1816, John VI became the king of the United Kingdom of Portugal, Brazil, and the Algarves, a region in southern Portugal.*

From the 1500s to the early 1800s, Brazil was a colony controlled by the country of Portugal. During that time, Portugal's king ruled Brazil. In 1822, Brazil gained independence from Portugal, and the country was ruled by an emperor. Brazil's first emperor was the son of the Portuguese king. In the late 1800s, after slavery ended, wealthy landowners forced the emperor from power. A republic was created, which allowed the citizens to vote for the country's leadership. Unfortunately, the republic didn't last forever, and **dictators** ruled Brazil. Brazil's dictatorship ended in 1985, when it became a republic once again. Today, the president serves a 4-year term, just like in the United States. He or she can serve two terms before a new president must be elected.

*The Brazilian federal judicial system contains labor, electoral, and military courts.*

## Branches of Government

Just like in the United States, the Brazilian government has three branches. The president and vice president represent the executive branch. In the legislative branch, officials help to make the country's laws. In the judicial branch, judges make sure the laws are interpreted and followed correctly.

# CHAPTER 3

# MEET THE PEOPLE

Brazil is often considered to be a melting pot. That means its citizens are a blend of people from all over the world, including Europe, Asia, and the Middle East. The diversity of its people makes Brazil a country rich with a wide variety of culture, food, and music.

The native people of Brazil are called Amerindians. They descended from many different native tribes that spoke different languages.

*In remote areas, students sometimes live very far from their school and have to walk a long distance to get there.*

*Although Brazil is a blend of many cultures, the influence of Portugal is the most widespread. Portuguese influences on Brazil include language, food, and popular customs.*

Portuguese explorers came to Brazil in the 1500s. They brought diseases with them that made Amerindians sick. They also took the native people as slaves. The Portuguese built plantations and then brought more slaves from Africa to work alongside the Amerindians on the land.

The Portuguese, Amerindian, and African people all began to blend together over time. People from other countries came to live in Brazil, as well. As a result, today Brazilians all look very different. Some Brazilians have light skin and eyes, while others have dark skin and features.

*In Brazil, groups of soccer fans called torcidas organizadas carry banners and lead chants during games.*

Brazil is one of only four countries in South America whose official language is not Spanish. The official language of Brazil is Portuguese. Around 98 percent of the country's population can speak Portuguese. Since so many people from other countries live in Brazil, it is common to hear people speaking many other languages there, including German and Spanish. Today, the country's native populations speak more than 274 different languages.

# ACTIVITY

Can you match the Portuguese words to their English translations? Hint: If you know any Spanish, you might have an easier time! See below for the answers.

| PORTUGUESE | ENGLISH |
|---|---|
| 1. Um (OOM) | a. Four |
| 2. Quatro (KWAH-troh) | b. One |
| 3. Cinco (SINK-oh) | c. Five |
| 4. Dois (DOYZ). | d. Three |
| 5. Três (TRAYZ) | e. Two |

*One type of Brazilian hummingbird makes the most high-pitched call of any bird.*

*answers: 1-b; 2-a; 3-c; 4-e; 5-d*

In Brazil, children of different ages are often in the same class together.

Children in Brazil must attend school if they are between 7 and 14 years old. Sometimes they continue to go to high school as teenagers to prepare for university, but it is not **mandatory**. Sometimes children from poorer families do not go to school at all. They stay home so they can help their parents earn money. Sadly, many other children in the country are homeless. They live on the streets and often do not attend school.

Poverty is a problem that affects many people in Brazil. Many people are so poor that they live in *favelas*, or **slums**. Many people in *favelas* live in shacks and don't have access to running water. In some places, children from poor families live on the streets instead of in homes. Their living conditions can be dirty and dangerous. Charitable groups work to help the homeless children of Brazil, but it is difficult to help everyone in need.

*About 6 percent of Brazilians live in* favelas *today.*

*Children in Brazil often learn how to play soccer on the streets or in dirt lots, instead of on a traditional soccer field.*

Kids in Brazil play many sports, with *futebol* being the most popular. *Futebol* is what Brazilians call soccer. After the 2016 Olympics, which were held in Rio de Janeiro, sports have become an important part of some schools' curriculums in Brazil. A program called Ginásio Experimental Olímpico is designed to help kids reach world-class levels in many sports before the 2020 Olympics in Japan. In this program, students' classes are a blend of traditional academics and their sport of focus.

In 2012, Neymar scored his 100th goal on his 20th birthday.

## 2018 World Cup

*Futebol* is wildly popular across Brazil. The national team has won the World Cup five times—more than any other country. In 2018, the Brazilian soccer team had a disappointing turnout at the World Cup, losing to Belgium in the quarterfinals. The soccer player Pelé was from Brazil, and many people think he is the best that has ever played the game. Today, the Brazilian soccer superstar Neymar is considered one of the most talented players in the world.

# CHAPTER 4

# CELEBRATIONS

Some of the world's most famous festivals and parties take place every year in Brazil, including Carnaval. Carnaval may be best known for people dressing up in bright costumes and feathered masks. Colorful floats are driven in parades, and many people even dance in the streets. The samba is a popular Brazilian dance you might see at Carnaval. Millions of people visit Brazil every year for the chance to experience Carnaval firsthand. Christmas is also popular in Brazil, where children hope to be visited by Papai Noel, the Brazilian version of Santa Claus.

*Elaborate Carnaval costumes can cost up to $10,000 U.S. dollars.*

*In Rio de Janeiro, Copacabana Beach's New Year's Eve party attracts up to 2 million people to celebrate and watch the fireworks.*

## HOLIDAYS AND CELEBRATIONS

January 1 **New Year's Day**

February or March **Carnaval**

April 21 **Tiradentes Day**

May 1 **Labor Day**

May or June **Corpus Christi**

September 7 **Independence Day**

October 12 **Nossa Senhora Aparecida** (The patron saint of Brazil)

November 2 **All Souls' Day**

November 15 **Proclamation of the Republic Day**

December 25 **Christmas**

# ACTIVITY

Create your own Brazilian Carnaval mask!

## MATERIALS:

- Flexible cardboard
- Pen or pencil
- Scissors
- Decorative items like sequins and colorful feathers
- Glue (and glitter glue)
- Popsicle sticks

## STEPS:

1. Cut out the cardboard in the shape of a carnival mask. Hold it up to your face and mark where eye holes need to be, then cut out two holes in those spots.

2. Glue the sequins, feathers, and any other decorative items onto the mask, making it as colorful as you'd like.

3. Glue the popsicle stick on the back of the mask, toward one edge, so that most of the stick hangs down below it.

4. Once all the glue is dry, use the popsicle stick as a handle to hold up the mask to your face!

Every year, groups of samba dancers create elaborate floats and dances. They compete for a cash prize of about $1 million U.S. dollars.

*Iemanjá Day is the largest Afro-Brazilian celebration in Brazil.*

Every December 31 in Rio de Janeiro, a celebration called *Iemanjá* honors the goddess of the sea. During this festival, people offer gifts by placing them on small boats in the ocean. Then they wait to see if the boats sink or return. Other popular holidays include Tiradentes Day, which honors Joaquim José da Silva Xavier, who led an unsuccessful **rebellion** for Brazil's independence. The day during which Brazilians celebrate independence from Portugal is September 7.

- Rio de Janeiro's Carnaval is the biggest celebration of its kind in the world.

- More than 500 street parties are held in the city each January through February during Carnaval.

- During Carnaval, more than 25,000 portable toilets are placed in the streets of Rio de Janeiro.

- Samba schools spend millions of dollars to prepare dances and floats for a competition that happens annually at Carnaval.

*Samba dancers practice their routines in special samba schools. There are over 100 samba schools in Rio de Janeiro.*

Although Rio de Janeiro's most famous beaches are often packed with people, there are quieter beaches on the city's outskirts.

The Portuguese brought Catholicism to Brazil, and now a majority of citizens are Catholic. Carnaval is one last big party every year before the observance of Lent begins. Lent is a period of time for prayer and fasting in preparation for Easter. During Lent, Catholics and other Christians make sacrifices in their daily lives to honor the sacrifice Jesus made when he took a 40-day journey into the desert. People that practice Lent might give up things they enjoy, such as candy or meat. Other religions practiced in Brazil include other forms of Christianity and Spiritism.

# CHAPTER 5

# WHAT'S FOR DINNER?

With a population blending South American, European, Asian, and Amerindian influences, it is no surprise that the food in Brazil can be just as diverse as its people. Brazilians use the natural bounty of the land and sea in their cooking. Foods like sweet potatoes, corn, and seafood are common ingredients. One of the most beloved dishes across Brazil is *feijoada*. This is a stew that usually has black beans, rice, and meat and is often served at family dinners. A fish stew called *moqueca* is typically served from a clay pot.

*Dinner time in Brazil is often a time to gather with family or friends at home, to talk about the day and enjoy a good meal together.*

*Some street markets in northern Brazil sell produce that comes directly from the nearby Amazon rainforest.*

Given the country's climate and vegetation, fruit is an extremely popular treat as well. A variety of fruit is featured in many foods and drinks, including the uniquely flavored guaraná soda. Guaraná is a fruit found in the Amazon rainforest. The most popular Brazilian fruit is perhaps açaí. Açaí is a hard purple berry that indigenous tribespeople often ate for energy. Nowadays, açaí is considered a superfood, meaning people around the world seek it out for its health benefits.

*Fruits of the açaí palm tree are enjoyed by many different animals and birds in Brazil's rainforests. These animals help to disperse the tree's seeds.*

*In Brazil, café da manhã translates to "morning coffee," or the first meal of the day.*

*Biriba fruit are also sometimes called wild sugar apples. The fruit is sweet and juicy.*

*Brazil is the fourth-largest producer of coconuts in the world today.*

For snacking, Brazil's *pão de queijo* is a delicious treat. Crunchy on the outside and soft in the middle, these cheesy rolls are made with tapioca flour, eggs, and *curado minas*, a type of cow's milk cheese. Similar decadent treats are *coxinhas*, little balls of fried batter filled with chicken. Sweet snacks Brazilians also enjoy are *biscoitos caseiros*, which are cookies made with condensed milk, sugar, and lots of butter.

## Snacks in Brazil

In Brazil, street food treats called *pastels* are sold everywhere from farmers' markets to *pastelarias*. *Pastels* are deep-fried dough pockets filled with a variety of delicious fillings. Beef, creamy hearts of palm, and cheese are some of the most common fillings found in pastels.

# RECIPE

*Quindim* is a very popular dessert in Brazil. It is a bright yellow custard that is sweet and dense, and very easy to make!

## INGREDIENTS:

- 1 cup (200 grams) of white sugar
- 1 cup (85 g) of shredded coconut
- 1 tablespoon (14.3 g) of butter, softened
- 5 egg yolks
- 1 egg white

## INSTRUCTIONS

1. Preheat the oven to 350 degrees Fahrenheit (175 degrees Celsius).

2. In a medium-sized bowl, mix the sugar, coconut, and butter. Stir in the egg yolks and egg white. Beat until well combined.

3. Pour into a 9-inch (23-centimeter) pie plate and place into a large roasting pan. Pour boiling water into the bottom of the roasting pan until the water reaches about halfway up the pie plate.

4. Bake about 30 minutes, or until golden brown on top.

5. Allow to cool completely, then turn out onto a serving dish and refrigerate before eating.

*Quindim can also be made in smaller individual portions.*

Lunches and dinners are considered times to socialize with family and friends in Brazil, while breakfast and morning coffee is more casual. Breakfast is simple and typically includes something like *pão francês* (French bread), which is sometimes eaten with ham and cheese. Lunch restaurants often offer per-kilo meals, where people pay based on how much food they put on their plates. At dinner time, rice and beans are a **staple** and are accompanied by meat or another main dish.

Between its diverse landscapes, wild animals, and busy cities, Brazil is a place meant for adventures. Walk along its beaches, tour its forests, or celebrate Carnaval—there's something for everyone in Brazil!

*For lunch, it's common for Brazilians to eat a hearty meal of rice, beans, a small amount of meat, a cooked vegetable, and a small salad.*

## Brazilian Steakhouses

Barbecued meat is commonly served in Brazil. It often comes in super-sized portions. *Churrascarias*, or Brazilian steakhouses, are places where cuts of meat are grilled over charcoal or wood.

# GLOSSARY

**deforestation** *(dee-for-uh-STAY-shuhn)* the cutting down of forests

**dictators** *(DIK-tay-turz)* people who have complete control of a government

**extinct** *(eks-TINGKT)* no longer living

**federal** *(FED-ur-uhl)* having to do with a system in which states have their own governments but are also united under one central power

**landlocked** *(LAND-lahkd)* surrounded by land

**mandatory** *(MAN-duh-tor-ee)* required

**manufacturing** *(man-yuh-FAK-chuh-ring)* the making of products, often with the use of equipment

**overpopulation** *(oh-vur-pahp-yoo-LAY-shuhn)* when too many people live in one area

**rebellion** *(rih-BEL-yuhn)* a fight or struggle against someone who is in control

**staple** *(STAY-ple)* a food that is eaten often

**slums** *(SLUHMZ)* very poor, crowded, and rundown housing areas in a city

**uninhabited** *(uhn-in-HAB-ih-ted)* not lived in

# FOR MORE INFORMATION

## BOOKS

**Gogerly, Liz.** *Journey Through: Brazil.* New York: Franklin Watts, 2018.

**Klepeis, Alicia.** *Brazil.* Exploring World Cultures. New York: Cavendish Square, 2017.

**Kortemeier, Todd.** *Explore Brazil.* Country Profiles. Mankato, MN: 12-Story Library, 2019.

## WEB SITES

### Britannica—São Paulo
*https://www.britannica.com/place/Sao-Paulo-Brazil*
Learn more about Brazil's capital city in this informative article by Britannica.

### Digital Dialects—Brazilian Portuguese Language Games
*http://www.digitaldialects.com/Brazilian%20Portuguese.htm*
Learn and practice Brazilian Portuguese words and phrases with these interactive games.

### National Geographic Kids—Brazil
*https://kids.nationalgeographic.com/explore/countries/brazil*
Explore facts on the geography, culture, and history of Brazil.

# INDEX

## ABOUT THE AUTHOR

Corey Anderson is a writer and editor based in the Los Angeles area. When not typing away at a computer, Corey enjoys exploring Southern California with her two sons and husband, and participating in running races and other athletic pursuits.